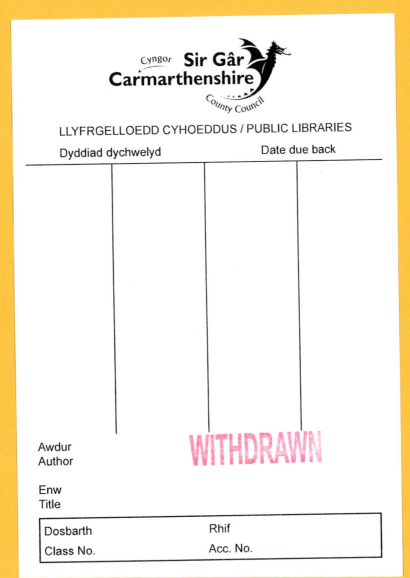

TOM JACKSON

NICK SHEPHERD

FOLLOW THE LINK

A JOURNEY THROUGH TECHNOLOGY

FROM FROGS' LEGS TO THE *TITANIC*...

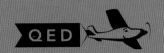

Quarto is the authority on a wide range of topics.

Quarto educates, entertains and enriches the lives of
our readers—enthusiasts and lovers of hands-on living.

www.quartoknows.com

Author: Tom Jackson
Illustrator: Nick Shepherd
Editors: Nancy Dickmann and Sophie Hallam
Designers: Adrian Morris and Sarah Chapman-Suire

Copyright © QED Publishing 2017

First published in the UK in 2017
by QED Publishing
Part of The Quarto Group
The Old Brewery, 6 Blundell Street
London, N7 9BH

A catalogue record for this book is available from the British Library.

ISBN 978-1-78493-777-5

Printed in China

MIX
Paper from
responsible sources
FSC® C016973

CONTENTS

INTRODUCTION

Did you know that when *Titanic* sank, the survivors were rescued because of a man who had made a dead frog's legs twitch all by themselves? That may sound completely crazy, but let's trace it back to the beginning.

SPARKS AND LIGHTNING

It turned out that the frog's legs wriggled for the same reason amber jewels made sparks, and that is why people tried to collect lightning inside glass jars. Some of them wanted to use it to bring the dead back to life. In the end, we made it into invisible waves that send our voices around the world – and that is how *Titanic's* crew sent out a distress call. How does any of this make sense? To find out, you have to follow the link…

IDEAS FROM THE PAST

The things we know about the world around us keep changing. What we know now is different to what people knew in the past, and in the future we will discover new ways of understanding how it all works. People in the future might think that our so-called 'modern' theories are just as far-fetched as we think the ancient Greeks' were! Discoveries do not come out of nowhere. Clever people figure out new things from what they know already – and they often get their ideas from very strange places.

AMAZING ELECTRICITY

This book tells the story of how we figured out what electricity is and how we learned to use it to communicate with each other. Over the centuries, we have taken the same power that creates a flash of lightning and used it to make Wi-Fi hotspots, power touchscreens and send video messages.

I DIDN'T KNOW THAT!

Along the way, you will learn that whale poo can be used in perfumes, electricity is named after fossilized tree resin, pylons were originally from ancient Egypt and particle accelerators were built to recreate cosmic rays coming from space. What else will we learn in the future?

The story starts in the middle of a lightning storm. Where will it it take us? Let's follow the link!

IN A LIGHTNING STORM

Lightning is the most powerful form of natural electricity on the planet. Just as we are today, ancient people were amazed by it — and a little frightened, too. Figuring out where it came from would change the world. Here's what we know now.

TAKING CHARGE

Lightning is formed when the electric charge of a cloud becomes different to the charge of the ground. A giant spark flies across the sky to make all the charges equal again. The charge is carried by tiny particles called electrons. The swirling air in a cloud makes the electrons gather in one part of it. The cloud is now electrically charged. There'll be a bolt of lightning soon!

SEVEN STRIKES, NOT OUT

During 35 years working as a park ranger in Virginia, USA, Roy Sullivan got hit by lightning seven times. (He also got attacked by bears 22 times!)

NATURAL POWER

Earth is struck by 44 lightning bolts every second. That's 1.4 billion a year! The energy in one bolt of lightning is enough to run a light bulb for three months.

DIRTY THUNDERSTORM

Lightning is not just seen in storms. The clouds of hot ash and smoke that billow from volcanoes also make lightning. It's known as a dirty thunderstorm.

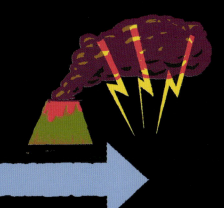

SUPERSONIC!

Thunder is the sound of lightning. The hot plasma swells up so fast it breaks the sound barrier just like a supersonic jet! We hear this as the rumble of thunder.

GIANT JUPITER

Space probes have seen lightning in clouds around other planets. A single bolt of lightning on Jupiter is longer than the whole of Britain!

JAGGED LIGHTNING

Air does not carry electricity very well. Lightning zig-zags around to find the easiest path, making the lightning look jagged.

WHAT NEXT?

Our understanding of lightning took centuries to figure out. To start with, people thought lightning was sent to Earth by angry gods!

A GOD'S HAMMER

Imagine living 2,500 years ago: the word *electricity* does not exist and no one knows about electrons, sound barriers or plasma. What would you think lightning was made of?

WEATHER GOD

In ancient India people believed that the Hindu god Indra was in charge of the weather. He sent the rain from heaven for the crops to grow. Indra rides on a white elephant and fires lightning bolts at his enemies using a rainbow.

SPARKS FROM A HAMMER

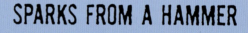

The Vikings believed that a rainbow was a bridge to the world of gods such as Thor, who bashed out bolts of lightning with his magical hammer. Thunder was the sound of Thor's hammer, and our word for it comes from the god's name.

DONNER AND BLITZEN

Santa Claus lives in Lapland, near to where the Vikings were from. Two of his reindeer are called Donner and Blitzen – which translates as Thunder and Lightning. Some stories say that Donner and Blitzen are Rudolph's mum and dad.

WORLD WAR II

Long ago, Vikings used a 'swastika' symbol to represent Thor's lightning. Today, however, we remember that shape as the symbol of the evil Nazis who took over much of Europe in World War II.

THE BLITZ

The Blitz was an attack on Britain by German bombers in 1940. London and other cities were bombed at night for nine months. One million houses were blown up and 40,000 people died. The word *blitz* is German for 'lightning', and referred to the lightning speed of the attacks.

THUNDERBIRDS

In parts of North America, some Native American tribes believed thunder was caused by the wingbeats of giant birds. In the American Pacific Northwest, some tribes make totem poles featuring thuderbirds because they protected humans by firing lightning from their eyes as they battled evil snakes that lived in the sky.

WHAT NEXT?

The ancient Greeks had other ideas about where lightning came from that did not involve the gods.

TRAPPED FIRE

The gods of ancient Greece, such as Zeus, Apollo and Aphrodite, behaved a lot like humans. They had big arguments and played silly games. So when it came to understanding lightning, Greek thinkers ignored the gods. Instead they used natural philosophy, or science.

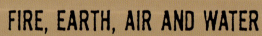

FIRE, EARTH, AIR AND WATER

Greek philosophers thought the world was made of four basic materials, or elements: fire, earth, air and water. They suggested that lightning was fire from the Sun that had been trapped inside wet air. During a storm, the air, water and fire all separated from each other, making wind, rain and lightning.

FIRE GOD

Empedocles was the first to write down the idea of the four elements. He thought he had uncovered a secret about the world that would make him live forever. To prove it, he jumped into Mount Etna, a huge volcano in Sicily. The plan did not work, though. Sadly, all that came out of the volcano were his metal shoe buckles.

FIFTH ELEMENT

The great philosopher Aristotle thought the Universe surrounding Earth was filled with a fifth element called ether. This idea was thought to be true for many centuries, and was used to explain how light could travel through empty space. It took the work of Albert Einstein to show that ether does not exist.

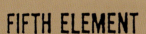

$$E = mc^2?!$$

IT'S QUINTESSENTIAL

Another word for ether is *quintessence*, from the word *quinta*, which means 'fifth'. 'Quintessential' can be used to describe a perfect example of something.

WHAT NEXT?

Greek philosophers studied an amazing material they called elektron. It was a strange orange stone, and rubbing it produced sparks like tiny flashes of lightning.

ALONG THE AMBER ROAD

The orange stone is called amber and it comes from resin that leaks from tree trunks. This sticky liquid gets buried underground and eventually becomes rock hard. The ancient Greeks called it *elektron*, which means 'droplet of sunlight'.

WHALE POO

Our word for amber comes from an ancient Persian term which actually means whale poo! Grey amber, or ambergris, is waxy stuff that washes up on beaches. It is the lining of the stomach of a sperm whale which it poos out occasionally. Ambergris is very rare and valuable. It is added to the best perfumes to give them a faint sweet smell.

FROZEN IN TIME

Some of the most highly prized amber jewels have insects and spiders trapped inside. These bugs drowned in the original resin and became frozen in time, unchanged over millions of years. Some people say it is possible to extract the DNA from these fossil animals – even the blood of dinosaurs they may have bitten. But DNA is very weak stuff and breaks up as the animal dies.

JEWEL TRADE

Amber has been used in jewellery for thousands of years. In Europe, amber was collected near the Baltic and North Seas and then taken south by merchants along a trade route called the Amber Road.

MUMMY'S JEWELLERY

King Tutankhamen, the most famous Egyptian pharaoh, was buried with jewellery made from large amber beads that had been brought all the way from the Baltic Sea.

THAT'S SHOCKING!

Amber does something very strange. If you rub it with a cloth, the amber attracts lightweight things like feathers, hair and dust. Amber even releases a spark – quite a shock! In the 1600s these effects were described as *electricity*, a word taken from the Greek term for amber.

WHAT NEXT?

Amber was not the only substance that had these properties. Another was sulphur, a material that was said to come from hell!

MAKING STATIC

In 1661, a German inventor called Otto von Guericke built a machine from a ball, or globe, of sulphur on a wooden stick. Spinning the globe with your hand had the same effect as rubbing a piece of amber – it became electrified.

FRICTION MACHINE

Von Guericke's machine was the world's first electrostatic generator. It used the power of friction to give an object static electricity. Static electricity is a build-up of charge, the same thing that is happening inside a storm cloud. The charge stays still – it is static – until it finds a way to escape and makes a spark.

OTTO VON GUERICKE
(1602–1686)

FLYING FEATHERS

Von Guericke found his globe attracted things in the same way amber did. He also saw that once an object – say, a feather – had stuck to his globe, he could make it fly off the globe by flipping it over. Electricity could push as well as pull.

SHOCKING FACTS

Friction between your shoes and a carpet charges up your body, just like von Guericke's machine. When you touch something metal, the charge escapes, giving you a tiny electric shock.

BURNING UP

Friction also makes things hot. When you rub your hands together, the friction warms them up. Air rubbing against a space capsule returning to Earth does the same thing, only it gets up to 1600 °C. One astronaut described re-entry 'like going over a waterfall in a barrel, but the barrel is on fire'.

FIRECRACKERS

Sulphur is one of the three ingredients of gunpowder, along with saltpetre and charcoal. Gunpowder was discovered by accident by Chinese wizards looking for a medicine that could cure all illnesses.

FIRE AND BRIMSTONE

Sulphur is one of the few elements found pure in nature. Lumps of it are found around volcanoes, giving them their acrid smell. Another name for sulphur is *brimstone*, which means 'burning rock'. When it burns, it turns into a blood-red liquid, and so ancient people assumed it must be what burns in the fires of Hell.

WHAT NEXT?

The English scientist Francis Hauksbee later built a copy of von Guericke's machine, using a ball of glass instead of sulphur. It didn't make sparks, but it glowed in the dark!

GLOWING GLASS

Francis Hauksbee worked at the Royal Society, a club for Britain's top scientists. It was his job to present the latest experiments to the leading scientists of the day. In 1705, he created the world's first light bulb — sort of!

FRANCIS HAUKSBEE
1660–1713

EMPTY VESSEL

To begin with, Hauksbee was more interested in another one of Otto von Guericke's inventions, a pump that could suck the air out of things. Hauksbee removed the air from inside a glass ball to find out what was left behind.

EERIE LIGHT

Hauksbee then used the empty glass ball in place of a sulphur globe to make electricity. It worked well, but Hauksbee noticed it did something else. He showed it off at a nighttime demonstration. All the candles were snuffed out and, in the darkness, he placed his hand next to the charged glass ball. The inside of the ball began to glow blue, first next to Hauksbee's hand and then all around the glass!

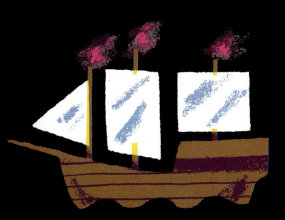

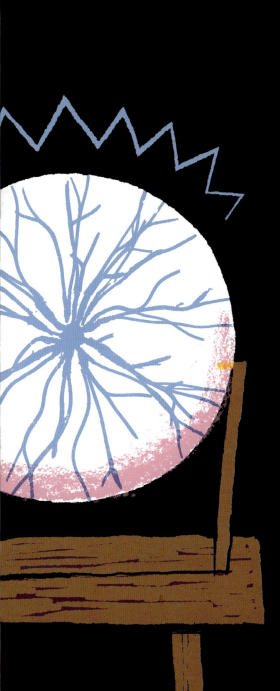

ST ELMO'S FIRE

Sailors would have recognized the glow inside Hauksbee's machine as St Elmo's Fire. This a weird violet light that appears at the top of a ship's mast during stormy weather.

PLASMA BALL

Plasma is the fourth state of matter, after solids, liquids and gases. If you heat a solid, it becomes a liquid, then a gas – and after that the gas atoms break apart and you get plasma. The Sun is a giant ball of plasma, and a comet streaking through the sky has a tail of plasma 500 million kilometres long!

IT'S MAGIC!

The glow was caused by electrifying small amounts of gas left inside the ball, turning it into plasma. But no one knew that at the time. Many people thought it was pure magic!

WHAT NEXT?

Hauksbee's invention proved very successful with a new type of performer: the electrician. Electricity was becoming a popular party trick!

AN ELECTRIC KISS

Electricians began using Hauksbee's generator in people's houses. However, they were nothing like today's electricians. In the 18th century, an electrician was a performer who showed off the amazing powers of electricity.

An electrician might even set the guests' alcoholic drinks on fire!

AFTER DINNER FUN

The best dinner parties would include an electrician show. The electrician would rub a glass rod with a silk handkerchief and then use it to make feathers fly up from the table as if by magic. He would also charge himself up using a generator and give the guests little electric shocks.

SILVER SPOONS

In Britain, before the 18th century people cut food with a knife and ate it with their fingers, or used a spoon. However, a wooden or cheap metal spoon made the food taste bad. Only expensive silver spoons did not affect the taste. (The steel ones we use had not been invented yet.)

If you were from a rich family, you might be 'born with a silver spoon in your mouth'.

SPARK OF LOVE

One of the most popular tricks was to ask a woman to stand on a stool with glass legs. She was then charged up, and a man – maybe her husband – would be asked to kiss her. As he got close, a spark would leap from her lips onto his, creating a truly electric kiss.

WIGGING OUT

In 18th-century Britain dinner parties were very grand affairs. Everyone dressed very smartly and both the men and the women wore wigs made from horse hair. They shaved off their real hair to avoid getting head lice, and kept their wigs clean with scented powder.

WHAT NEXT?

Scientists were not interested in magic shows. They wanted to know more about electricity. In the 1730s an English schoolteacher decided to investigate by suspending a schoolboy from the ceiling!

19

THE FLYING BOY

Stephen Gray's first job was as a dyer, using chemicals to add colours to fine cloth. He was fascinated to see that silk threads would produce sparks as they rubbed against each other when woven on a loom.

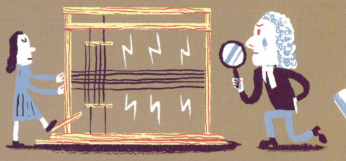

STEPHEN GRAY
1666–1736

TRAVELLING CHARGE

Gray noticed that he could attach things to his charged glass tube to make it longer – and the electrical effects still worked. He created a 240-m long cable made from twisted hemp fibres. He hung it from silk threads and found that an electric charge at one end travelled all the way to the other end!

FREE OF EARTH

Gray had to make sure the charged object was not 'earthed' by touching the ground. He built a wooden cradle that hung from silken ropes and asked a boy to lie in it. Gray then charged the boy using a Hauksbee machine. The cradle was lowered closer to the ground which was littered with gold leaf. The gold started to flutter around the boy, sticking to his body then flying off again.

Gray called this experiment 'The Flying Boy'.

WORM MATERIAL

Silk is made from the cocoons of 'silkworms', which are actually caterpillars of a moth that eats mulberry leaves. The material, which is strong but lightweight, was invented in China about 5,000 years ago.

ELECTRIC SHOW

Gray became a teacher in a London orphanage, instructing the boys living there all about science, including electricity. He charged up glass tubes, just like the showy electricians did, and used them to attract feathers and flakes of gold foil.

COLOURED CABLES

Today's electric wires are made from conductors and insulators as described by Stephen Gray. The copper wire is the conductor, which carries the electricity. The metal is surrounded by plastic insulator, which stops the current leaking out.

FLOWING FLUIDS

Gray thought electricity was an invisible liquid that flowed from one object to another. The Flying Boy showed that some substances conducted electricity. Other stuff stopped the flow.

WHAT NEXT?

If electricity was a strange liquid, perhaps it would be possible to hold some in a bottle or jar?

BOTTLING ELECTRICITY

Until the 1740s, only small amounts of electrical charge could be made — and they soon escaped back to the Earth as a little spark. Then an accidental — and near deadly — discovery changed all that.

POURING CHARGE

In 1745, a scientist called Pieter van Musschenbroek, working in the Dutch city of Leyden, tried to 'pour' electricity into a glass jar. He ran a wire from a generator into a jar filled with water. He put the jar on an insulating wax mat to stop the charge escaping. However, nothing happened.

Why isn't anything happening?

PIETER VAN MUSSCHENBROEK
(1692–1761)

GLASS

We've been keeping liquids in glass bottles for around 5,500 years. The ancient Egyptians invented glass by melting sand until it became a gooey hot liquid that could be shaped before it cooled hard.

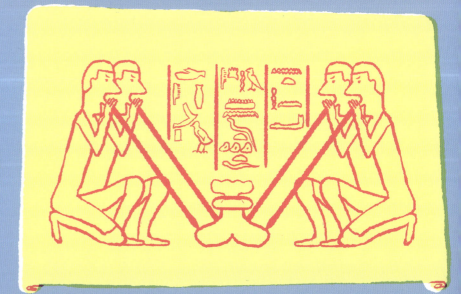

BIG SHOCK

Forgetting to use the mat, Musschenbroek charged the jar again while holding it in his hand. When he touched the top, a huge electric shock threw him across the room! Luckily he survived, and repeated the process, only this time he used a metal rod to connect the outside of the jar to the wire that ran inside. This created a bright spark. Musschenbroek's device became known as the Leyden jar. It was the first device for storing electricity.

BETTER DESIGN

An improved version of the Leyden jar replaced the water with metals. The jar had a metal rod on top connecting to a chain that hung down inside. The jar was covered in metal foil, inside and out. The charge lasted for weeks, and was released in a mighty jolt by connecting the outside foil to the metal rod.

FLATTENED

Metal is malleable, meaning it can be hammered or rolled into flat foil sheets. Gold is the most malleable metal of all. One gram of gold can make 1 square metre of ultrathin foil. It would take 261g – about the weight of 4 eggs – to cover a tennis court in gold!

WHAT NEXT?

It took many years to understand how it worked, but something like the Leyden jar is used in almost all our electrical equipment today — and perhaps in ancient ones, too.

VOLCANIC GLASS

Obsidian is a natural glass formed by the heat of volcanic eruptions. When cracked, it creates a very sharp edge. Some surgeons still use knives made from obsidian.

TAKING CHARGE

A Leyden jar is a type of capacitor. A capacitor's job is to store a current and then let it out all in one go. These devices are used in mobile phones, computer circuits and televisions. The latest electric cars use immense 'super-capacitors'.

CHARGING UP

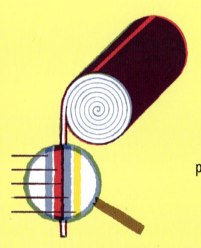

A capacitor has two layers of conducting material, separated by a layer of insulating material. Early Leyden jars had foil on the inside and the outside. A modern capacitor has two layers of metal foil separated by a thin plastic film. These layers are rolled up tightly like a Swiss roll.

ELECTRICAL POWER

According to the Old Testament, Moses built the Ark of the Covenant to hold the Ten Commandments. It was believed that God's spirit was also carried inside. The Ark was a wooden box covered inside and out by a layer of gold. Does this sound familiar? Legend said that lightning flashed between the statues on top, and if anyone touched the Ark they would die. The Ark could have collected an electric charge from hot desert winds whistling past it, creating the amazing effects.

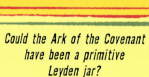

Could the Ark of the Covenant have been a primitive Leyden jar?

SAY CHEESE!

Unlike a battery, a capacitor usually releases its stored energy very quickly. For example, the flash on a camera needs to produce a huge burst of light in a split second, so it uses a capacitor. The capacitor takes a few seconds to charge up by taking energy from the camera's batteries. Then, when you take the photo, all that energy is released quickly as the bulb flashes.

THEREMIN

One of the first electronic musical instruments was the theremin, invented in 1928. Players create eerie music without even touching it. The two thick wires sticking out of the instrument each make up half of a capacitor. The player's hands make up the other side of the capacitor. By moving their hands, the player controls how much charge is in the capacitors and that changes the tone and volume of the sound.

WHAT NEXT?

Although they could see its effects, no one understood what was actually inside a Leyden jar. A French scientist convinced 200 monks to help him find out more.

25

SHOCKING SPEED

In 1746, Jean–Antoine Nollet, a French scientist, was interested in measuring how fast electricity travelled through things. His method involved connecting 200 monks together, and the results were a shock for everyone.

Ouch! That hurt!

Ready, steady, go!

JEAN–ANTOINE NOLLET
(1700–1770)

LINING UP

Nollet's idea was to send the electricity from a Leyden jar from one monk to the next. Each monk would jump at the powerful shock. When lined up, the 200 helpers made a conductor that was about 1.6 kilometres long. How long would it take for the last monk to feel the electricity? The monks held metal wires, which allowed the electricity to move between them easily. The men were arranged in a circle, so Nollet could see when the first monk in the chain got a shock and when the last one did.

MONK OR MONKEY?

Some groups of monks wear a brown cape with a hood. In Italian, this outfit is called a *cappuccio*. In the 15th century, explorers in South America discovered a type of monkey with a tuft of brown fur on its head. It reminded them of a monk's hood, so the monkeys were named capuchins. A pale brown milky coffee – a cappuccino – is named for the same reason.

SPEED OF LIGHT

A pure copper wire conducts electricity at just below the speed of light, but electricity would have moved through the monks a bit more slowly - at about half the speed of light. Albert Einstein explained in 1905 that the speed of light is the speed limit of the entire universe. Not even electricity can go that fast.

IT'S SHOCKING!

To his amazement, when Nollet connected the chain of holy men to his Leyden jar, they all leapt up in shock at the same time. The electricity had whizzed around the circle so fast it was impossible to say which monk had jumped first!

WHAT NEXT?

Nollet's monk experiment sounds like a made-up story, but it's probably true. However, there is a much more famous story from the history of electricity that may have been made up.

CAPTURING LIGHTNING BOLTS

Benjamin Franklin was one of the first American scientists and later became a Founding Father of the United States. In the 1750s, he suggested that lightning — thought at the time to be a magical mystery of nature, or even a sign from God — was actually a gigantic electric spark.

THOUGHT EXPERIMENT

In 1750, Franklin had a bright idea. He said that a tall metal pole connected to a Leyden jar would attract lightning during a storm. The lightning would charge the jar in just the same way as a generator did.

BENJAMIN FRANKLIN
(1706–1790)

LIGHTNING CONDUCTOR

Franklin's idea led to the invention of the lightning conductor. All tall buildings have them today to carry lightning safely to the ground. Lightning normally hits the tallest thing around – which is why you should never sit under a tree during a lightning storm.

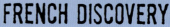

FRENCH DISCOVERY

Franklin never put his idea to the test, but the Comte de Buffon had a go. He used an empty wine bottle, but it still worked. After the storm, an assistant approached the bottle, and a big spark leapt to his hand, burning the skin.

FLYING A KITE

A legend grew that Benjamin Franklin had attracted lightning with a key hanging from a kite. If this had really happened, Franklin would have been killed. But the story may be partly true – he may have used the key to collect charge building up in the air as a storm brewed.

CLEVER FELLOW

The Comte de Buffon also tried to measure the age of Earth and was the first person to suggest animals evolved into new species – 100 years before Charles Darwin! His brain is now in the base of a statue in Paris's Museum of Natural History.

A NEW WORD

Benjamin Franklin invented the word *battery*, meaning a store of electricity. He got the idea from several Leyden jars all wired together, which looked like a battery of cannons.

WHAT NEXT?

So Benjamin Franklin showed that electricity was at work in nature. Soon another scientist proved that electric currents were at work inside our bodies as well.

29

FROM DEAD FROGS TO A LIFE FORCE

In the 1780s, an Italian doctor named Luigi Galvani showed that electricity was more than just sparks and flashes of light. He had found that electricity seemed to come out of bodies as well.

Electricity must be what makes animals alive!

LUIGI GALVANI
(1737–1798)

SPARKY FROGS

One day, Galvani was cutting up a dead frog and pinned its legs to a table with a metal hook. Then his knife touched the hook by accident. There was a spark and the frog's leg moved! Galvani tried to recreate the effect by hanging frogs' legs on railings connected to a lightning conductor. He thought a bolt of lightning would make the legs move. But they twitched even when there was no lightning!

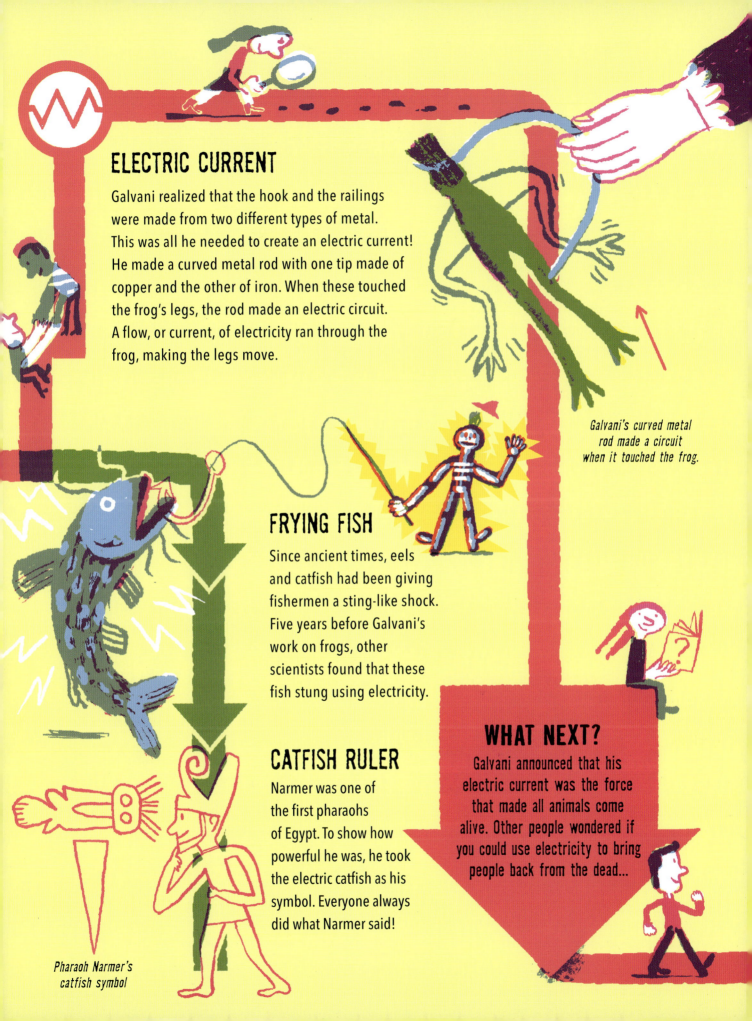

ELECTRIC CURRENT

Galvani realized that the hook and the railings were made from two different types of metal. This was all he needed to create an electric current! He made a curved metal rod with one tip made of copper and the other of iron. When these touched the frog's legs, the rod made an electric circuit. A flow, or current, of electricity ran through the frog, making the legs move.

Galvani's curved metal rod made a circuit when it touched the frog.

FRYING FISH

Since ancient times, eels and catfish had been giving fishermen a sting-like shock. Five years before Galvani's work on frogs, other scientists found that these fish stung using electricity.

CATFISH RULER

Narmer was one of the first pharaohs of Egypt. To show how powerful he was, he took the electric catfish as his symbol. Everyone always did what Narmer said!

Pharaoh Narmer's catfish symbol

WHAT NEXT?

Galvani announced that his electric current was the force that made all animals come alive. Other people wondered if you could use electricity to bring people back from the dead...

ZOMBIES!

Galvani had a nephew called Giovanni Aldini. Aldini travelled the great cities of Europe showing off what his uncle's life–giving electrical discovery could do. His performances sparked the imagination in many ways.

MEGA MONSTER

The idea that electricity could make life was the inspiration behind the famous sci-fi story, *Frankenstein*. The author Mary Shelley describes how a doctor (this is the actual Frankenstein) created a monster by sewing body parts together, and then brought it to life with a bolt of lightning.

FAMOUS MUM

Mary Shelley was one of the first women to become a world-famous writer. Her mother was also famous. Her name was Mary Wollstonecraft and she spent her life demanding that women and men be treated equally.

BACK FROM THE DEAD?

In London, in 1803, Aldini was given a dead body from the city's prison. He used electricity to make the man's eyes blink and have his face pull scary expressions. The audience was terrified!

FRANKENCAT

A German scientist, Karl Weinhold, replaced a dead cat's brain with a mixture of metals. He said that the electricity from the metal made the cat walk around – although no one really believed him.

ELECTRIFIED PEOPLE

Frankenstein's monster was made up, but millions of people are alive today thanks to electricity. Tiny gadgets called pacemakers are fitted to their hearts to make them beat better using an electrical pulse.

Pacemakers are about the size of a matchbox.

WHAT NEXT?

Alessandro Volta found a way of making currents without any animals at all. His invention, the electric battery, would change the world all over again...

A PILE OF POWER

An Italian chemist, Alessandro Volta, was not convinced by the idea that electricity was a special life force. He showed that electricity could be made in other ways.

TASTY CLUE

Volta got an idea when he put copper and silver coins together on his tongue. They created a tingle which, Volta said, was a tiny flow of electricity.

ALESSANDRO VOLTA
(1745–1827)

TONGUE TALE

You may have heard that sections of the tongue pick up different flavours: the tip detects sweetness, the back part picks up bitter flavours, while salty and sour tastes are collected at the sides. This is not true. The whole tongue can pick up all kinds of tastes – including a fifth 'meaty' taste called umami.

IMPRESSED EMPEROR

Volta's pile was the first version of what we now call a battery. Volta showed his invention to Napoleon Bonaparte, who ruled most of Europe at the time. Napoleon was so impressed he made Volta a count.

MODERN BATTERIES

Today's batteries use lithium chemicals, which are made from chemicals collected from salt flats in South America. The largest one is Salar de Uyuni in Bolivia, which is also the flattest place on Earth.

MAKING A PILE

Volta made a larger amount of electricity by building a pile of metal discs, soaked in acid. The acid formed a chemical link between the metals, which allowed electricity to flow up the pile. Volta connected wires to the top and bottom and, instead of a spark of electricity, his electric pile produced a continuous flow.

WHAT NEXT?

Volta's battery changed the world — it would lead to electric lights, heaters and motors. But first a huge battery was used to split up molecules.

DOING THE SPLITS

In 1808, a brash young English scientist called Humphry Davy built the largest battery the world had ever seen, in the cellars of the Royal Institution, a new research centre in London. This massive battery was 800 times stronger than Volta's original.

HUMPHRY DAVY
(1778–1829)

LAUGHING GAS

Davy made his name with his research on 'laughing gas'. This gas is nitrous oxide, a combination of nitrogen and oxygen. When Davy breathed it in, it made him go numb all over – and start to giggle. Laughing gas became the world's first breathable painkiller. It is still used by dentists and doctors today.

LET THERE BE LIGHT

One effect of Davy's huge electricity supply was very spectacular. Davy attached thick graphite wires to each end of his battery, and then brought them close to each other. A blinding arc of light filled the gap, creating a constant stream of what looked like lightning. Named the arc lamp, this system was used for the first electric streetlights.

CHEMICAL ADVENTURES

Davy knew that electricity could make chemical reactions run in reverse. Water is made from hydrogen and oxygen, but electrifying it turned it back into two separate gases. Davy used this technique on other materials, such as lime and potash. Davy's experiments revealed the unknown elements – such as sodium, potassium, calcium and chlorine – that these materials were actually made of.

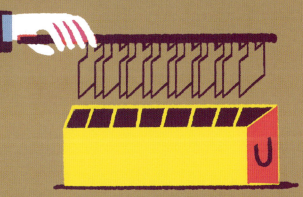

Davy's enormous battery was made from hundreds of copper and zinc plates.

CLEAN CHEMICAL

Chlorine is used to sterilize (clean) water, and it is chlorine that gives swimming pools their distinctive smell. The smell shows that the chlorine is working – but the stronger the smell, the dirtier the water!

DAVY LAMP

Humphry Davy was a hero to miners. Flames from their oil lamps often caused deadly explosions from gas escaping from the coal. Davy invented a safety lamp with a copper grill to stop the flame from escaping.

WHAT NEXT?

Humphry Davy became famous for his amazing demonstration – he was the world's first celebrity scientist. The next great electrical discovery would be made during a public display.

ELECTRICITY MEETS MAGNETISM

Today we know that electricity is just one part of a much wider area of science called electromagnetism. This connects electricity to magnets as well as to light, heat and many kinds of invisible rays. That connection was made completely by chance.

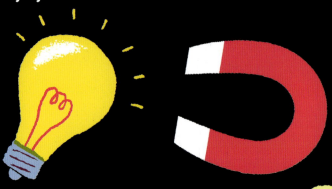

DOING THE SWING

In 1820, the Danish scientist Hans Christian Oersted was showing his students how electricity made a wire warm up and glow. He happened to have a compass on his desk, and during the demonstration, everyone saw the needle swing toward the electrified wire. Oersted had discovered electromagnetism: electric currents turning things into magnets.

HERO METALS

The word *magnet* comes from Magnesia, a kingdom in ancient Greece that was ruled by King Magnes. This area is full of lodestones – rocks that are natural magnets.

GENERATOR

This type of generator is now called a Faraday wheel.

If electricity makes magnets, could magnets make electricity? In 1831 Faraday showed that they did, and that moving a wire near a magnet makes an electric current run through it. Faraday built a machine that did the opposite of his motor: the spinning magnet created electricity. This was the first electric generator.

MAGNETIC NORTH

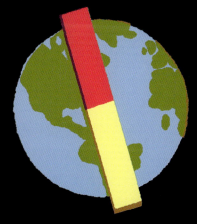

GILBERT'S GLOBE

Scientists already knew that Earth was a giant magnet. This is why compasses always point north – they are attracted to our planet's magnetism. This was figured out in 1600 by William Gilbert, who also invented the word *electricity*.

MAGNETIC SOUTH

MOTOR MEN

Humphry Davy and his friend William Wollaston thought they could make an engine that used electricity and magnets to make motion. But Michael Faraday (Davy's assistant) was the one who actually managed it! In 1821 he made a simple machine where a wire spun in a circle around a magnet. This was the first electric motor.

WHAT NEXT?

While Faraday was linking electricity and magnets, other researchers were more interested in a link between electricity and light.

FLAMES AND FLICKERS

In the 1850s, two German researchers began to study light and colour, and how they were linked to the elements. One set fire to elements, while the other electrified them!

ROBERT BUNSEN (1811–1899)

The Bunsen burner created clean flames where the colour was easy to see.

FLAME TESTER

Robert Bunsen has a famous name – he invented the gas burners used in laboratories. Bunsen studied how different chemicals burned with flames of specific colours: potassium burns purple, lithium is red, while magnesium is white.

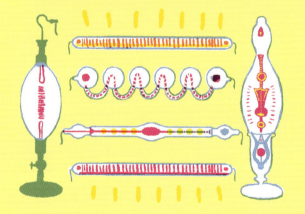

GLOW STICK

Around the same time, Julius Plücker was trying a slightly different experiment. He put tiny amounts of an element inside an empty glass tube. When it was electrified, it glowed with colour. Different elements glowed with different colours.

COLOUR SIGNATURE

Every element – from gold to carbon – produces a unique set of colours when it is heated up. An atom of a particular element can take in energy. When the atom gives the energy out again, it is released as coloured light. This discovery was the starting point of the branch of science called quantum physics.

SUN GAS

Astronomers saw the colours of hydrogen, sodium and other chemicals in the light from the Sun. In 1868, Norman Lockyer saw a set of unknown colours – he had discovered a new element! He named it helium, after the Greek sun god Helios.

STRETCHED LIGHT

The light from stars showed astronomers that familiar elements were spread all over the universe. But the colours in starlight were all redder than expected. As light waves travel towards us, they get stretched, making the colours look redder. This shows that the stars are moving away from us – meaning that the Universe is expanding.

HELIUM CORE

GAS BULBS

Gases in tubes form the basis of today's fluorescent bulbs. These bulbs contain mercury gas, which emits invisible ultraviolet light. The coating on the inside of the bulb turns the ultraviolet light into the light that we see.

WHAT NEXT?

An American inventor realized that electric lights would be something everyone wanted. He invented a different kind of light bulb – and set about changing the world.

WAR OF THE CURRENTS

Inventors soon discovered a better type of light bulb: the incandescent bulb, which used a burning filament. But without mains electricity, it would be useless. The famous inventor Thomas Edison came up with a way for these bulbs to light up a city.

THOMAS EDISON
(1847–1931)

BRIGHT IDEA

Edison knew that no one would buy his light bulbs if there was no way to power them. So his General Electric Company also built power stations in New York and other cities to supply the electricity for these lights.

DIRECT CURRENT

Edison's system sent direct current (DC) along underground cables. It could only travel a few kilometres before fading away, so many power plants were needed. George Westinghouse had a system that used alternating current (AC). This carried power much further, so one huge power plant could supply many towns.

RESISTANCE

An incandescent light bulb glows because the electricity struggles to run through the wire, or filament, inside. The wire resists electricity, which turns the current into heat and light.

Edison's electric system was safe, but not very efficient.

CURRENT COMPETITION

In the 1880s, Edison and Westinghouse went to war to win customers. Edison said that Westinghouse's use of overhead wires was very dangerous. But Westinghouse won the battle and today the world's power supply still uses his system.

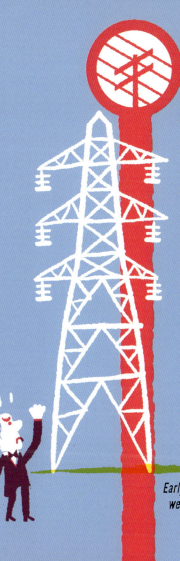

Early overhead wires were not insulated very well.

ELECTROCUTION

To show the deadliness of AC, Thomas Edison used it to kill animals by electrocution – even an elephant called Topsy! These demonstrations led to the invention of the electric chair, a machine for executing criminals.

AC/DC

Electricity is not a stream of particles flowing through a wire. Instead, it is a wave of ripples that passes through a soup of electrons in the metal. In a direct current, the wave travels in one direction, but in an alternating current, the wave switches direction back and forth hundreds of times a second.

WHAT NEXT?

George Westinghouse did not actually invent the AC power supply system himself. That was done by one of the most ingenious – and mysterious – inventors of all time.

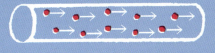
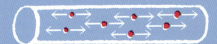

Unlike DC, AC can travel in either direction.

43

MAGICAL MISTER TESLA

Westinghouse's electrical supply system (which we still use today) was based on an invention by a Serbian genius called Nikola Tesla. Tesla went on to invent many things that were ahead of their time – and some still are!

BIG PUSH

The AC supply system can be sent across hundreds, even thousands of kilometres in high-voltage cables. High voltage means there is a huge force pushing the electricity along. However, this high-voltage supply is so powerful that it would make a TV, washing machine or computer explode! We need to keep it carefully controlled.

NIKOLA TESLA
(1856–1943)

TRANSFORMATION

Tesla invented a voltage controller called a transformer. A step-up transformer boosts the voltage at the power plant, before it is sent out. A step-down transformer lowers the voltage and sends a useful-sized current to your house.

ADAPTER

The big plug on some gadgets is called an adapter. Its job is to convert an AC supply into a DC one. It blocks any current that is going the wrong way, so only a DC supply gets through.

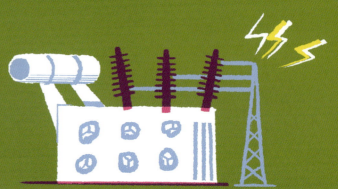

TESLA COIL

Tesla also invented a coil which could be charged up to make bolts of artificial lightning. In 1901, Tesla built a giant one near New York City to send coded electrical pulses through the ground. He believed he could tap into natural electric currents deep inside the planet to make a communications system. Unfortunately, it didn't work. Today, Tesla coils are mainly used for special effects by performers.

SAFETY FIRST

Even the low-voltage current in the home is powerful enough to kill, especially when it touches wet skin. That is why we have to be so careful with electrical appliances in the bathroom and other areas of the home.

ELECTRIC BATH

Tesla also invented Cold Fire, a high-voltage 'dry washing' system. The bather stood on a plate electrified with thousands of volts. As long as he didn't touch the ground he was safe, but the germs on his skin were blasted away by the 'electrical fire' surrounding him!

WHAT NEXT?

Tesla changed the world but did not have a happy life, dying alone and forgotten. Another great scientist, James Clerk Maxwell, is also largely unknown, but some call him the Scottish Einstein.

MAKING SOME WAVES

James Clerk Maxwell wrote his first scientific paper at the age of 14 and by 24 he was a university professor. This brainy Scot's biggest discovery was linking electricity and magnets to light.

INDIGO!

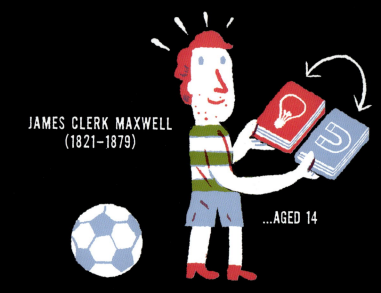

JAMES CLERK MAXWELL
(1821–1879)

...AGED 14

SEVEN COLOURS

Isaac Newton first described the rainbow as red, orange, yellow, green, blue, indigo and violet. He included indigo because he thought the number seven was magic. The word *orange* had arrived in Europe in the 16th century along with the orange fruit. Before that the colour was known as *geoluread*, or 'yellow-red'.

BENEATH RED

In 1800, William Herschel split sunlight into its colours, then measured their temperature. He found that red light was hot, but the colourless area beyond that was even hotter. He had found invisible rays, now known as infrared. Our skin feels these rays as heat.

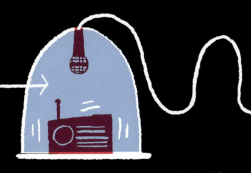

NOTHING!?

VIBRATIONS IN NOTHING

One of the mysteries of the 19th century was how light could travel through a vacuum when sound waves couldn't. Maxwell explained that light was a weird vibration that goes from side to side in an electric field and up and down in a magnetic one.

SPEED OF LIGHT

Maxwell calculated that light always travelled at the same speed. No one could understand how that was possible. Wouldn't light from a high-speed train move faster than light from a street lamp? It took Albert Einstein to explain how time can slow down and speed up, but light always travels at the same speed!

MEASURING COLOURS

Every wave is measured by its wavelength – the distance from one crest to the next. The wavelengths of light waves are incredibly tiny. Our eyes detect the different wavelengths as colours. Red light has long wavelengths; blue has short ones. Maxwell suggested that there were other waves with wavelengths our eyes could not see.

SPEED OF LIGHT

299,782,458 m/s

WHAT NEXT?

In 1886, twenty years after Maxwell had set out his ideas, a German used a pulse of electricity to produce some invisible waves. These waves now whizz across the sky and criss-cross our homes.

ON RADIO

What's that you say? You've never heard of Heinrich Hertz? Well, you should have. This German discovered radio waves, and we now measure their frequencies — in fact the frequency of any wave — in hertz.

HEINRICH HERTZ
(1857–1894)

INVISIBLE WAVES

Maxwell had suggested that electricity running through a wire would create ripples of electromagnetic waves around it. If the current was powerful enough, could we possibly see those waves as light? Hertz set out to find them.

CREATING SPARKS

Hertz made one electric coil spark by electrifying another one. Amazingly, this even worked when there was no wire between them! Hertz knew that this must be the effect of the invisible waves. He built new machines to transmit and receive them.

BEATEN TO IT

An English scientist, Oliver Lodge, had figured out these waves before Hertz, but went on holiday before telling anyone. When he got home, Hertz had become famous for his amazing discovery. Oops!

MICROWAVES

The wavelength of a radio wave is anywhere from 1 mm to 100 km, and the shorter wavelengths are called microwaves. Microwaves can heat up the water and fats in food. That's why we use them in microwave ovens.

COSMIC MICROWAVES

In 1964, astronomers found microwaves coming from all over the sky. This radiation is the faint glow of the Big Bang! The waves began as a flash of ultra-hot energy and were squashed inside a universe that was much smaller than now. Over billions of years, those waves have been stretched, turning them into long, cold radio waves.

WATCH THE GAP

Hertz's and Lodge's machines both used a 'spark gap,' a small space between wires that created a spark when electrified. The receiver's spark was very faint. Hertz spent most of a year in a dark room looking for the tiny flashes. These invisible waves were named Hertzian waves in his honour. We know them today as radio waves.

WHAT NEXT?

Many people saw the possibilities of using invisible waves for communication. A young Italian would be the man who led the way to this wireless world.

GOING WIRELESS

By the 1890s, making mysterious Hertzian waves was easy enough, but converting them back into electricity was a lot harder. If that problem could be cracked, then the waves could be used for an astounding new invention: wireless communication.

GUGLIELMO MARCONI
(1874–1937)

GOT YOU!

OVERSEAS

Radio waves travel best over water, because there are no forests or mountains to get in the way. Marconi's wireless telegraphs were fitted to ocean liners, sending signals between ships and to the shore.

TRANSATLANTIC TIP-OFF

In 1910, a doctor called Hawley Crippen poisoned his wife and escaped from England on a ship. However, the captain spotted him and used the ship's radio to call the police. Dr Crippen was arrested when he reached Canada. His story was the first international criminal manhunt.

WIRELESS WHIZ

Many engineers tried to build communications systems that used radio waves. A young Italian called Guglielmo Marconi built a 'wireless telegraph' for the British Post Office, though he copied someone else's system – it was poor old Oliver Lodge, again! Marconi's system could send Morse code messages. In 1901, he sent one from England to Canada, a distance of 3400 km! To do that, the radio waves had to bend around Earth's curvature.

ATOM SMASHERS

Cosmic rays travel almost as fast as light. They hit the air so hard that they smash the atoms apart. To get a closer look at how this worked, scientists recreated these collisions inside huge machines called particle accelerators. The biggest one, the Large Hadron Collider in Switzerland, is 27 km long – large enough to surround an international airport.

ELECTRIC ATMOSPHERE

A German scientist, Victor Hess, went up in a balloon and found that the air became more electrified the higher he went. This was because cosmic rays from space were smashing into the air. That created an electrified layer high in the sky, and Marconi's signals were bouncing off it as they travelled around the world.

WHAT NEXT?

Thanks to wireless communications, people crossing the Atlantic Ocean were no longer cut off from the world. A tragedy at sea would show just how important that was.

A TITANIC RESCUE

On 10 April 1912, the ocean liner *Titanic* set sail from England to America. It was one of the fastest and most luxurious ships in the world, and its designers boasted that it was unsinkable!

WARNING RECEIVED

Titanic had a Marconi radio system. The radio signallers' main job was to send messages on behalf of wealthy passengers. When *Titanic* was sailing through the cold Atlantic Ocean near Canada, they received warnings from other ships about dangerous icebergs. But they were too busy sending out the passengers' messages to pay much attention.

CALLING FOR HELP

On the night of 14 April, *Titanic* hit an iceberg and started to sink. The radio operators sent out distress signals, becoming the first to use the signal 'SOS'. It is sometimes said that this message stands for 'Save Our Ship' or 'Save Our Souls'. In fact, it is just a very easy signal to send by Morse code – and to hear. Morse code uses patterns of short dits and long dahs for each letter. SOS is dit-dit-dit dah-dah-dah dit-dit-dit.

DAH–DAH–DAH–DIT–DIT–DIT

24-HOUR RULE

Ever since the sinking of *Titanic*, it has been the law that every ship has its radio on 24 hours a day.

DISTRESS CALLS

The word 'Mayday' is used as the main distress call today. It sounds like *m'aider*, which is French for 'help me' and is easy to hear over a radio. If the emergency is not so dangerous, people use the distress call 'pan-pan' – from *panne*, which means 'breakdown' in French.

TRAGIC CONSEQUENCES

When *Titanic* began to sink, *SS Californian* was close enough to see its lights in the distance. However, the radio operator on *Californian* had turned off his radio, so the ship did not pick up the distress signal. The first rescuers arrived a few hours later. Sadly, 1,500 people had already died, but without those radio signals many more would have perished in the cold ocean.

WHAT NEXT?

Titanic's radio messages were sent in a simple code. However, the race was on to send voices over the airwaves.

CRYSTAL CLEAR

Early radio systems could only detect simple coded patterns. To transmit voices, a more precise system was needed.

IRON FILINGS

FILING SYSTEM

Early radios picked up signals by using iron filings – tiny grains of metal. The tiny electric current made by a radio signal made the filings all cling together. The filings acted like a switch connected to a loudspeaker, which made buzzes in a pattern that matched the radio signal's code.

LOUDSPEAKERS

A loudspeaker turns electric current into a wave in the air – or sound. It has an electromagnet inside a permanent magnet. A current from a radio receiver turns the electromagnet on and off very quickly, so it is pushed and pulled by the other magnet, creating a wobble motion. That wobble moves the speaker's cone, which vibrates the air, making sounds.

BETTER VIBRATIONS

In the 1900s, scientists experimented with electrifying crystals. They found that a crystal radio worked much better than using iron filings – well enough to transmit voices and music.

CRYSTAL

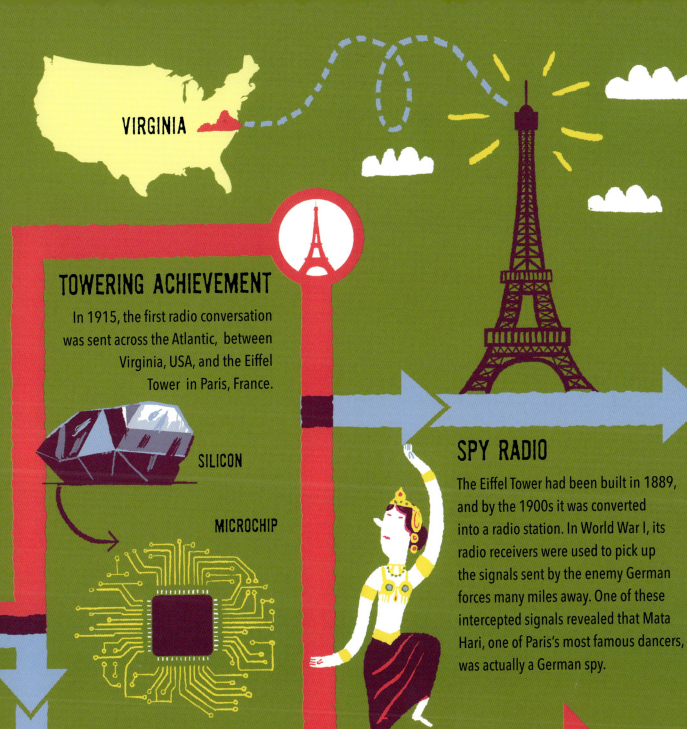

VIRGINIA

TOWERING ACHIEVEMENT

In 1915, the first radio conversation was sent across the Atlantic, between Virginia, USA, and the Eiffel Tower in Paris, France.

SILICON

MICROCHIP

SEMICONDUCTOR

The crystals used in radios were semiconductors. They let a current run in one direction but not the other, so the electric signal coming through was always clear. The crystals all contained silicon which is used today to make the microchips inside computers and phones.

SPY RADIO

The Eiffel Tower had been built in 1889, and by the 1900s it was converted into a radio station. In World War I, its radio receivers were used to pick up the signals sent by the enemy German forces many miles away. One of these intercepted signals revealed that Mata Hari, one of Paris's most famous dancers, was actually a German spy.

WHAT NEXT?

Radio systems became powerful enough to broadcast signals, which meant many people could pick up the signals all at the same time. And soon the signals were sending more than just sounds.

PICTURES AROUND THE WORLD

If radio signals could carry sound, why not pictures, too?
That was the thought of many inventors in the early 20th century.

SPACE AGE TV

The first communications satellite, *Echo 1*, was a house-sized metal balloon that was launched in 1960. Its shiny surface reflected radio signals from the ground. By 1962, radio waves carried the first live TV pictures between America and Europe. The signal was sent via the new Telstar satellite.

ELECTRON

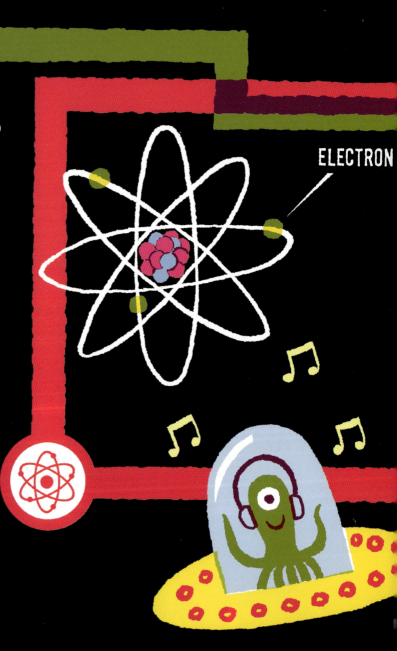

SUBATOMIC PARTICLES

Electrons had been discovered and named in 1899 by J.J. Thomson, who used a cathode ray tube. He showed that the glowing 'ray' was in fact a stream of tiny charged particles. He calculated that they were thousands of times smaller than an atom. They were the first subatomic particles to be discovered.

The first inventor to succeed was John Logie Baird. In 1926, he transmitted a moving image of a face using radio, then converted it back into a picture. It was very crude, made up of about 900 dots of light – compared to two million in a modern TV!

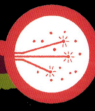

PUPPET TIME

Baird's camera could not pick up a real face, so the first TV show starred a brightly painted puppet called Stooky Bill.

BRIGHT DOTS

By the late 1930s, TVs used cathode ray tubes, similar to Julius Plücker's glowing gas tubes. The tube sent a flickering beam of electrons across the back of a screen, making a pattern of dots that changed so fast it made a moving image!

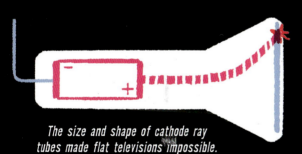

The size and shape of cathode ray tubes made flat televisions impossible.

WHAT NEXT?

While sound and pictures sent by radio were connecting more people than ever, for person-to-person chats we've mostly been using a very different system.

EARTH CALLING

Our radio waves have been leaking out of Earth since the 1930s. However, these signals would be impossible to detect in space. In 1974, scientists sent the first radio signal designed to be heard by aliens. We've not heard back from them yet...

MAKING CONNECTIONS

In 1876, Alexander Graham Bell spilt acid on himself. He needed help from his assistant in another room. 'Watson, come here. I want to see you!' he said. These were the first words spoken on Bell's latest invention: the telephone.

ALEXANDER GRAHAM BELL
(1847–1922)

DOWN THE LINE

The word *telephone* means 'distant voice', and Bell's system carried voices as an electric current along a wire and turned them back into sound. As is common in the history of invention, his system was not the first. In 1861, a German called Johann Reis had sent his voice down a wire. To test the system, he said, 'The horse does not eat cucumber salad.' However, only he heard it. There was no one else on the line!

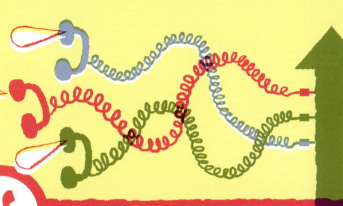

PHOTOPHONE

Bell had his own idea for a wireless communication system in the 1880s. Instead of radio waves (which hadn't been discovered yet), Bell's 'photophone' sent messages as beams of light. The sound waves made a mirror vibrate, and that created a flickering light signal. The invention was a hopeless failure, but modern optical fibres do something similar by sending messages along glass wires as flashes of laser light.

MAKING EXCHANGES

In the early days, each of Bell's telephones had to be connected directly to another. Some people had several phones, each connected to a different friend. By the 1900s, everyone's phone was connected to the local telephone exchange. An operator connected callers to different lines by plugging in the wires. Sometimes they got the wires tangled and you ended up talking to the wrong person. Even today, when two people are talking and not understanding each other, one might say: 'We've got our wires crossed.'

AHOY!

HELLO!

RIVAL IDEAS

Bell thought telephone users should answer the phone by saying, 'Ahoy!' Thomas Edison proposed using 'Hello'. Before the telephone, 'hello' was not a greeting, but an expression of surprise. Hello, fancy that!

WHAT NEXT?

Over the years, the telephone has steadily changed in many ways, but our 'phone' is still the most important communication device we own.

DIALLING WITH BEEPS

In the 1920s, phone lines were given numbers for the first time. The connection system counted out the number being called as a series of clicks – 1 click for 1, 9 for 9 and 10 clicks for a 0 – and then you would be connected to the right telephone.

SPIN THAT WHEEL

Today, even though we are actually pressing buttons, we still talk about 'dialling a number'. That term refers to the numbered wheel – called a dial – which was used on old telephones. To dial, you put your finger into a numbered hole in the wheel and turned it all the way to a stop point. Then you let go, and the wheel spun back, producing a set of clicks for the number you'd selected.

LEGACY LANGUAGE

We still use other bits of old telephone language. To end a call, we press a button on the phone, but we say we've 'hung up'. The mouthpiece of early phones were hung on a hook, which disconnected the line.

AREA CODES

Every telephone number is unique, but only the last digits relate to a particular line. All the numbers before that are area codes telling the system the country, city and exchange that the telephone is part of. In American movies, all telephone numbers begin with 555, a fake code that has been reserved for pretend numbers.

Some area codes cover a huge space, while others are much smaller.

LISTEN CAREFULLY

A phone's tones are actually made up of two notes. The high note indicates the row of the button being pressed and the lower one indicates the column, so all 12 buttons (0 to 9,* and #) have a unique pair of tones.

TOUCH TONES

In 1963, a new system was introduced that used a keypad. Instead of clicks, each key produces a tone of a certain pitch. Dialling a number became much faster – and a bit more musical, too!

WHAT NEXT?

All communication is digital today, and it was the phone network that led the way with digital technology.

GOING DIGITAL

Every form of communication is digital nowadays. But what does that even mean? A 'digit' is a single number, so at its simplest a digital message is made up of numbers.

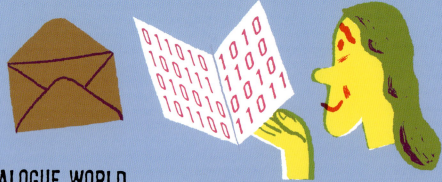

ANALOGUE WORLD

Before digital, communication was analogue, which meant it was copying the natural world. A pure musical note is made from a sound wave that does not change its wavelength, and an electrical or radio signal transmitting that note would do the same. A complex sound, such as a voice, is a jumble of rising and falling wavelengths, and the analogue signal would be jumbled in the same way.

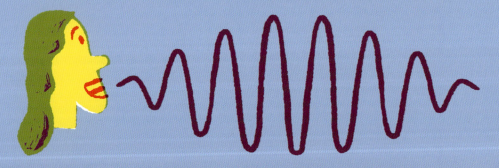

TIDE PREDICTOR

In 1872, Lord Kelvin built an analogue machine with wheels, cogs and levers for calculating the times of tides. You turned the handle to represent the motion of the Earth, Sun and Moon, and the machine produced the times of high and low tides. It worked so well that the Norwegian coastal service used one for the next 100 years!

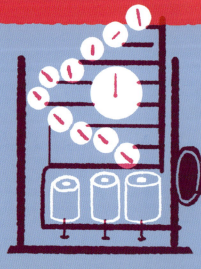

BREAKING IT DOWN

A digital signal breaks up the analogue world into tiny slices and then gives each slice a fixed value. To transmit a digital signal, you send all the values of the slices and put them in the right order. It looks (or sounds) just like the original. Digital signals are more efficient because they use less information.

ANALOGUE SIGNAL

DIGITAL SIGNAL

ON OR OFF?

Digital signals are transmitted not in normal numbers, but as 1s and 0s. These are instructions for the tiny semiconductor switches inside computers. A 1 tells the switch to be on, and the 0 turns it off.

BITS OF INFORMATION

Each digit in this system is called a bit. Early computers were programmed to work with 8 bits at a time, and 8 bits was termed 1 byte. Half a byte, or 4 bits, is called a nibble.

0101110

WHAT NEXT?

Numbers that use just ones and zeroes are called binary numbers, and they do a lot more than send signals. They can be used to make decisions, too.

DIGITAL MOTHERLAND

The world centre for digital technology is Silicon Valley in California. An inventor called William Shockley moved there in 1956 to be nearer to his mother – and then set up one of the world's first microchip factories.

SILICON VALLEY

ONLY LOGICAL

Computers, mobile phones and tablets work using digital technology which is made up of millions — perhaps billions — of tiny switches called transistors. Each switch can do just two things: it can be on or off, but never in between.

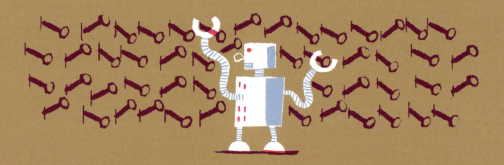

PROCESSING PLACE

The computer's 'brain' is its processor. Each transistor in the processor receives bits of information – a '1' bit is a pulse of electric current, and a '0' bit is no current. The transistor then converts that into a new bit.

$$0 + 0 = 0$$
$$0 + 1 = 1$$
$$1 + 1 = 1$$

WIRED WEIRD

Transistors make new bits by doing very simple sums using just two digits. But they follow a weird set of rules where the answer is always 1 or 0. So $0+1 = 1$ and $0+0 = 0$, but $1+1=1$ as well! Each transistor is a kind of logic gate. It is built to do a particular calculation, such as adding or multiplying the inputs or swapping them for the opposite number. Whatever answer comes out is sent to the next transistor.

GATEWAYS TO LOGIC

Transistors are made from silicon mixed with other chemicals like arsenic and germanium. Different chemicals are placed on a small chip of pure silicon: a microchip. Microchips are integrated circuits, so there are no wires involved. Every component is connected because it is one small part of the same chip of silicon.

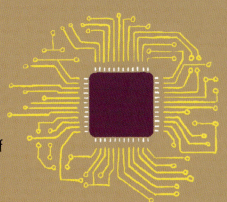

IMPORTANT POISON

Before being used in high-tech silicon chips, the main use of arsenic was as a poison, used mostly by gardeners to kill bugs and pests – but also by murderers! The gold paints used in Renaissance art also contain deadly arsenic.

TOTALLY CHILLED

The mathematics used by computers was invented in 1847 by George Boole, from Cork, Ireland. One cold, rainy day, after the long walk home from his university job, he ended up in bed with a fever. His wife decided to cure this illness by using what caused it, so she poured buckets of cold water over him. He died within a week, aged just 49.

WHAT NEXT?

Inventors had given us clever computers, telephones and broadcast systems. Why not connect them all together?

COMMUNICATION NETWORK

In 1940, an American engineer figured out a way to control an early computer down a telephone line. This was the first computer network. Today we have the Internet, which is a network of computer networks. It connects more gadgets than there are people on Earth.

PROTECTION NEEDED

The Internet was invented by the US military. They wanted to make sure important communications kept working in a war. Just one broken phone line might disconnect many bases. So they invented a system where messages travelled in small packets that found their own way through a network. If one route did not work, a packet would try another.

ALL ABOUT @

Electronic mail, or email, was developed for use on the Internet. Messages were addressed with a name and a domain, which showed where that person was connected. The two are separated by an @ sign. This symbol was invented long ago as a quick version of the French word 'à', which means 'at'.

STAYING CONNECTED

The Internet still uses old copper telephone lines, as well as a faster method called fibre optics. This uses flexible glass tubes that carry signals as flashing laser lights. Each message travels at the speed of light.

SPARKLING SYSTEM

Fibre optics use a system in which the laser reflects off the inside instead of leaking out of the glass fibre. This is also what makes a diamond sparkle. The light reflects around inside and then shines out the top, making the jewel glitter brilliantly.

SWITCHED ON

In 1969, the Internet system only connected a few universities. By the 1990s, the world's telephone networks were being hooked up. Telephone lines carry electrical versions of sound waves, and computer data is sent in the same way. It is turned into high-pitched sound and then sent as a telephone signal.

WHAT NEXT?

With everyone connected, communication is easier than ever, but that also means it is harder to keep things private. Hack alert!

PHREAKS AND GEEKS

Most people who use a phone and computer for sending messages and talking to friends have no idea how it works. However, hackers do know, and they use their skills to steal information.

PRIVATE LINE

Internet messages are encrypted, or turned into a code. The codes use a very large number made by multiplying two smaller ones. To send your friend a message, you could make a code number and send it to her. She would use it to encrypt her messages. Anyone can steal her message, but they must know your two starting numbers to read it. It would take a computer centuries to figure them out. However, you have the right numbers and can decode your friend's message straightaway.

2, 3, 5, 7, 11, 13, 17, 19, 23...

PRIME NUMBERS

The small numbers used for encrypting messages are prime numbers. A prime number is very special because it can only be divided by itself or the number 1. The biggest prime found so far has more than 22 million digits.

BLOW THE WHISTLE

Before there were computer hackers, there were phone phreakers. A phreaker takes over a phone system using secret codes. The first phreaker was the American John Draper. Draper got a toy whistle in a cereal box, which made the same tones as the telephone control system. By blowing it into his phone, Draper got free calls!

STAR AND HASH

As well as numbers, a telephone has a star key and a hash key. These were originally added for sending commands to the telephone control system, but we use them in other ways today. The hash symbol is a tag to help when searching the Internet – #searchforthis. The proper name of the hash symbol is the octothorp.

COLOURED HATS

Hacking skills can be used for good as well as bad. Black hat hackers are the criminals, while white hat hackers work to protect computer networks. In old black and white Western movies, the hero always wore a white cowboy hat, while his enemies had black hats.

WHAT NEXT?

The communication revolution began with radios and telephones, then moved to computers. Now we are using radios and telephones again.

SMART SCREENS WITH SOFT KEYS

Telephones today are nothing like the ones your parents grew up with. Those had wires and could only make and receive calls. Modern phones can go anywhere, and do a lot more!

A cell tower can be installed on a roof, a pylon or even up a fake tree!

CELLULAR NETWORK

A mobile phone is actually a radio. However, the radio signal does not travel directly between callers. It is picked up by a cell tower and then sent to the cell tower nearest to wherever the other caller is.

HANDHELD COMPUTER

A modern phone can also handle emails, text messages, videos, Internet access and navigation information. Although they are very different to us, to the phone these things are all the same – just a series of 1s and 0s.

VIKING KING

Mobile phones communicate over short distances using the Bluetooth radio system. It is named after Harald Bluetooth, a Viking king who brought people together, just like the radio system brings telephones and computers together.

TOUCH INTERFACE

No one wants to attach a keyboard, mouse and screen to their phone. Instead, the screen does it all. The screen is a capacitor (remember those?) and when you touch it, a tiny electric current leaks into your finger. This tells the device where you are touching. The screen then displays what you need, whether it is buttons, soft keys – or just the latest cat video!

LIQUID CRYSTALS

A smartphone screen uses a liquid crystal display. A liquid crystal is a chemical that blocks light when it is electrified but lets it pass through when it is not. The smartphone screen electrifies these chemicals in a pattern that creates the same pattern of light and dark dots for you to see.

WHAT NEXT?

Radios are everywhere, and not just in our phones! We even have little radio stations in our homes.

DIGITAL CAMERA

A smartphone camera has 8–24 megapixels, so each photo has 8–24 million coloured dots. The Extra Large Telescope in Chile, opening in 2024, has a camera with more than 3 billion pixels!

A WIRELESS WORLD

Radio connections mean we no longer need wires to communicate. The future will definitely be wireless!

Today we get great sounding music from our phones, computers and digital radios.

WHY WHAT?

Before mobile phones, before personal computers and before the Internet, every family wanted a Hi-Fi. This stood for High Fidelity, meaning 'very faithful', and music coming from a Hi-Fi was the best you could get. Now, instead of Hi-Fi, we all want Wi-Fi. That doesn't really stand for anything, but it turns your house into a wireless computer network.

ALL TOGETHER

Wi-Fi is provided by a router. This connects to the Internet, then broadcasts a radio signal that fills your house. You can connect anything to the Wi-Fi signal: your phone, TV, computer, e-reader, games machines, central heating – and of course the Hi-Fi too! The router connects these devices to each other as well as to the Internet.

EDISON
GOLD MOULDED
RECORDS

ECHO ALL
OVER THE WORLD

CAPTURING MUSIC

The first recording machines stored music on wax cylinders. Next they used shellac discs. Shellac is a plastic made from crushing up sap-sucking insects called lac bugs.

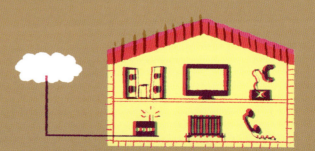

INTERNET OF THINGS

Today we are building the IoT or the 'Internet of Things'. The Internet used to just connect computers and phones, but soon everything from fridges, traffic lights and cars to shops and buses will be connected.

I think you should call 999!

INTERNET TOILET

One day your toilet may be connected to the Internet. It could use the seat to weigh you and sensors to analyse your wee and poo. It might then tell the fridge to buy healthier food – or even call an ambulance in an emergency!

WHAT NEXT?

Why stop here? Let's take a look at what the future might hold.

LOOKING FOR BLACK HOLES

Wi-Fi works because it can untangle the jumble of radio waves that are bouncing around inside the house. The way it does this was invented in 1996 by the Australian engineer John O'Sullivan.

LOOKING TO THE FUTURE

We have come a long way since our ancestors thought thunder and lightning came from gods battling in the heavens. But there is still more to discover and invent.

MIND INTERFACE

The first clue about how electricity runs in currents came from the study of frogs' legs and muscles. Our brain runs on electricity, too. We can see the electrical activity of the brain using a machine called the electroencephalograph (EEG). Perhaps one day our brains will link to the Internet! There is already technology that uses the electrical activity from thinking to control objects outside our body. Someday soon, electrical technology may allow us to communicate telepathically through the Internet.

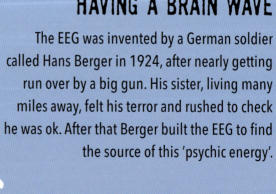

HAVING A BRAIN WAVE

The EEG was invented by a German soldier called Hans Berger in 1924, after nearly getting run over by a big gun. His sister, living many miles away, felt his terror and rushed to check he was ok. After that Berger built the EEG to find the source of this 'psychic energy'.

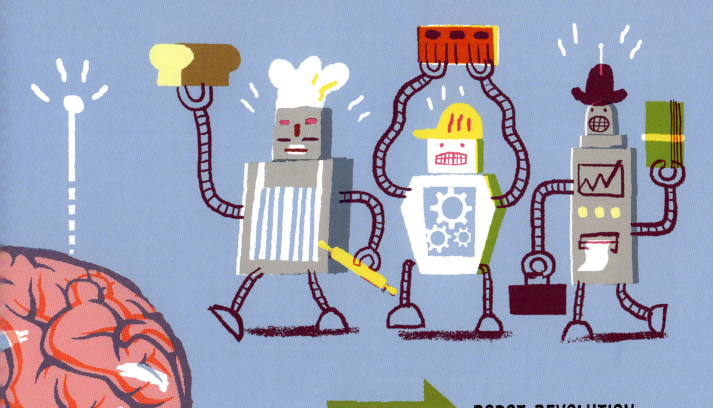

ROBOT REVOLUTION

The Internet of Things will create huge amounts of information, creating a new field of science called Big Data. Big Data will make it possible to make intelligent computers. These will not be like robot versions of humans. Instead they will do just one job, but do it really well without ever needing a break.

ROBOT REPRESENTATIVE

In the days of *Titanic*, people had to travel to do business – despite the dangers. In the wireless world, we could use robots to replace us in distant places. Your face appears on the robot's screen and you control its movements around an office, a friend's home, even at a party – just as if you were there.

WHAT NEXT?

So, there we have it. Radio waves, electricity, magnetism, light. These are all part of the same natural phenomenon, called electromagnetism. We've been studying it for 25 centuries and what we learned changed the world completely. Now it's time to find the next link. Where do you think it will go?

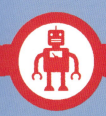

TIMELINE

Here is a reminder of all the links that we've followed so far. Do you think that you might work out the next link in the chain?

Beginning of time: Lightning strikes!

Bolts of lightning are huge sparks of electricity made during storms. It took a long time to figure out what they were made of.

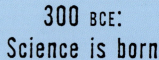

300 BCE: Science is born

Greek philosophers reasoned that lightning is fire escaping from air. Natural philosophy, or science, is born!

1799: The first battery

Alessandro Volta builds a metal pile that can make currents using chemistry. This is the world's first battery.

1780: Bringing dead frogs back to life?

Luigi Galvani finds that a dead frog's legs move when electricity flows through them. Scientists think that electricity might be the thing that makes animals alive. Could it bring the dead back to life?

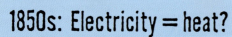

1850s: Electricity = heat?

Electrifying elements produced colourful lights – and burning them made the same coloured flames. This shows that light and heat are linked to electricity as well.

1862: Making connections

James Clerk Maxwell figures out that light and heat are waves, and predicts there are other kinds of invisible rays.

1880s and 1890s: Using radio waves

Heinrich Hertz uses an electric spark to produce invisible radio waves, and Guglielmo Marconi develops a system for sending messages with them over long distances.

1661: The first electrostatic generator

Otto von Guericke produces powerful sparks by rubbing a ball of sulphur, rather than amber.

1705: The world's first light bulb (sort of!)

Francis Hauksbee replaces the sulphur ball with a glass globe – which glows in the dark when electrified.

1745: Storing electric charge

Pieter van Musschenbroek collects the electric charge made by a Hauksbee generator inside a glass jar – named after the Dutch city of Leyden.

1740s: Conducting and insulating

Stephen Gray uses Hauksbee's machine to electrify a boy. It shows that some materials carry, or conduct, electricity, while others block it, or are insulators.

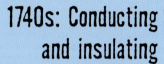

1950s onwards: Going digital

Converting communication signals into numbers, or digits, makes it possible to send a lot more information at once. Computers are connected through the telephone network to create the Internet.

Present day: What's next?

We now have devices that combine the technology of telephones, radios and computers to send and receive digital information of all kinds. Where will that take us next?

GLOSSARY

acid a chemical that reacts with metals and rocks

alternating current an electric current that switches direction dozens of times a second

amber fossilized tree resin

analogue a quantity that can increase and decrease continuously, unlike a digital quantity which rises and falls in fixed steps

astronomer a scientist that studies the stars and planets

atmosphere the blanket of gases that surrounds a planet or moon

atom the smallest possible unit of a substance

battery a device for storing an electric current

capacitor a device for storing electric charge

charge something certain types of material can have that makes them produce sparks or electric currents

circuit a ring of wire or another conductor that allows an electric current to flow through it

compass a magnetic device that always points north

conduct to carry an electric current

conductor a material that easily carries an electric current

current a continuous flow of electric charge through something

digital using numbers or digits to describe something

direct current a type of electric current that always flows in one direction

earth to release dangerous electric charges or currents to the ground, making them safe

electricity a natural process that creates sparks or currents

electromagnetism the area of science that investigates electricity and magnetism

electron a negatively charged particle found in all atoms. Most electricity is created by electrons moving around.

element a simple material that cannot be split up into simpler ingredients

encrypt to turn into a code

fossil a part of an animal or plant that has been turned to stone over millions of years

friction the force that makes substances rub against each other instead of sliding past one another smoothly

generator a machine for making electricity

graphite a soft form of pure carbon that is used in pencil leads

hemp a plant with fibres that can be used to make cloth

insulator a material that blocks electric currents

Leyden jar an early type of capacitor, used to collect large charges

magnetic field the force field around a magnet

malleable able to be easily hammered or rolled flat. Some metals are very malleable.

microchip a set of tiny circuits arranged on a single piece, or chip, of silicon

molecule a group of atoms that are bonded together to make a particular substance

monk a holy man

motor a machine that converts electricity (or another source of energy) into motion

obsidian a dark natural glass made by volcanic eruptions

orphanage a home where children without parents can be looked after

pacemaker a small machine that provides electric pulses that keep the heart beating

philosopher a thinker who tries to work out answers to questions about life and the world

plasma a hot gas that has become electrically charged

radioactive having atoms that fall apart, releasing energy

resistance a measure of how hard it is for electricity to flow through a substance

satellite an object that orbits another larger object in space. Some satellites, such as moons, are natural, but we have also launched many artificial satellites into space.

semiconductor a material that can switch from being a conductor of electricity to being an insulator

silk a fine fibre made by insects and spiders. Silk fibres can be woven into a soft fabric.

static electricity a build-up of electric charge that is released as a spark

sulphur a yellow element

telegraph a system for sending coded messages along wires

transformer a device that controls the strength of an electric current

transistor a switch made from a semiconductor

transmitter a device that sends out radio waves

vacuum a space with nothing in it, not even gas

wavelength the distance from the peak of one wave to the next peak in front (or behind)

INDEX